Indiana
Total Eclipse Guide

Official Commemorative 2024 Keepsake Guidebook

2024 Total Eclipse State Guide Series

Aaron Linsdau

Sastrugi Press

Copyright © 2019 by Aaron Linsdau

All rights reserved. No part of this book may be reproduced or transmitted in any form or by any means, electronic or mechanical, including photocopying, recording, or by any computer system without the written permission of the author, except where permitted by law.

Sastrugi Press / Published by arrangement with the author

Indiana Total Eclipse Guide: Official Commemorative 2024 Keepsake Guidebook

 The author has made every effort to accurately describe the locations contained in this work. Travel to some locations in this book is hazardous. The publisher has no control over and does not assume any responsibility for author or third-party websites or their content describing these locations, how to travel there, nor how to do it safely. Refer to local regulations and laws.

 Any person exploring these locations is personally responsible for checking local conditions prior to departure. You are responsible for your own actions and decisions. The information contained in this work is based solely on the author's research at the time of publication and may not be accurate in the future. Neither the publisher nor the author assumes any liability for anyone climbing, exploring, visiting, or traveling to the locations described in this work. Climbing is dangerous by its nature. Any person engaging in mountain climbing is responsible for learning the proper techniques. The reader assumes all risks and accepts full responsibility for injuries, including death.

Sastrugi Press
PO Box 1297, Jackson, WY 83001, United States
www.sastrugipress.com
 Quantity sales: Special discounts are available on quantity purchases by corporations, associations, and others. For details, contact the publisher at the address above.

Library of Congress Catalog-in-Publication Data
Library of Congress Control Number: 2018914098
Linsdau, Aaron
Indiana Total Eclipse Guide / Aaron Linsdau-1st United States edition
p. cm.
1. Nature 2. Astronomy 3. Travel 4. Photography
Summary: Learn everything you need to know about viewing, experiencing, and photographing the total eclipse in Indiana on April 8, 2024.

ISBN-13: 978-1-64922-315-9 (paperback)

508.4—dc23

All photography, maps and artwork by the author, except as noted.

10 9 8 7 6 5

Contents

Introduction	4
All About Indiana	6
Overview of Indiana	6
Weather	11
Finding the Right Location	13
Road Closures and Traffic	14
Wilderness and Forest Park Safety	15
Eclipse Day Safety	17
All About Eclipses	19
Total vs Partial Eclipse	20
Early Myth & Astronomy	22
Contemporary American Solar Phenomena	24
Future American Eclipses	26
Viewing and Photographing the Eclipse	27
Planning Ahead	28
Understanding Sun Position	29
Eclipse Data for Selected Locations	31
Eclipse Photography	31
Eclipse Photography Gear	34
Camera Phones	36
Viewing Locations Around Indiana	43
Remember the Indiana Total Eclipse	65

Introduction

Thank you for purchasing this book. It has everything you need to know about the total eclipse in Indiana on April 8, 2024.

A total eclipse passing through the United States is a rare event. The last US total eclipse was in 2017. It traveled from Oregon to South Carolina. The last American total eclipse prior to that was in 1979!

The next total eclipse over the US will not be until April 8, 2024. It will pass over Texas, the Midwest, and on to Maine. After that, the next coast-to-coast total eclipse will be in 2045.

It's imperative to make travel plans early. You will be amazed at the number of people swarming to the total eclipse path. Some might say watching a partial versus a total eclipse is a similar experience. It's not.

This book is written for Indiana visitors and anyone else viewing the eclipse. You will find general planning, viewing, and photography information inside. Should you travel to the eclipse path in Indiana in April, be prepared for an epic trip. The estimates based on the 2017 eclipse suggest that millions will converge on Indiana.

Some hotels in the communities and cities along the path of totality in Indiana have already been contacted by people to make reservations. Finding lodging along the eclipse path may be a major challenge.

Resources will be stretched far beyond the normal limits. Think gas lines from the late 1970s. It may be likely that traffic along highways will come to a complete standstill during this event. Be prepared with backup supplies.

Many smaller Indiana towns are far from any major city. Indiana country roads can be slow. Please obey posted speed limits for the safety of everyone. Be cautious about believing a map application's estimate of travel time in Indiana.

People in communities along the path of the total eclipse may rent out properties for this event. With this major celestial spectacle in the spring of 2024, be assured that Indiana "hasn't seen anything yet."

Is this to say to avoid Indiana or other areas during the eclipse? Not at all! This guidebook provides ideas for interesting, alternative, and memorable locations to see the eclipse. It will be too late to rush to a better spot once the eclipse begins. Law enforcement will be out to help drivers reconsider speeding.

Please be patient and careful. There will be a large rush of people from all over the world, converging on Indiana to enjoy the total eclipse. Be mindful of other drivers on eclipse weekend, as they may not be familiar with Indiana roads.

You should feel compelled to play hooky on April 8. Ask for the day off. Take your kids out of school. They'll be adults before the next chance to see a total eclipse over America. Create family memories that will last a lifetime. Sastrugi Press does not normally advocate skipping school or work. Make an exception because this is too big an event to miss.

Wherever you plan to be along the total eclipse path, leave early and remember your eclipse glasses. People from all around the planet will converge on Indiana. Be good to your fellow humans and be safe. We all want to enjoy this spectacular show.

Visit www.sastrugipress.com/eclipse for the latest updates for this state eclipse book series.

Author Information

Polar explorer and motivational speaker Aaron Linsdau's first book, *Antarctic Tears*, is an emotional journey into the heart of Antarctica. He ate two sticks of butter every day to survive. Aaron coughed up blood early in the expedition and struggled with equipment failures. Despite the endless difficulties, he set a world record for surviving the longest solo expedition to the South Pole.

Aaron teaches how to build resilience to overcome adversity by managing attitude. He shares his techniques for overcoming adrenaline burnout and constant overload. He inspires audiences to face their challenges with a new perspective. As a motivational speaker, Aaron talks about courage, resilience, attitude, safety, and risk. He hopes that you will be inspired and have an enjoyable time watching the total eclipse in Indiana.

Visit his websites at www.aaronlinsdau.com or www.ncexped.com.

All About Indiana

OVERVIEW OF INDIANA

Indiana, the Hoosier state, or the "Crossroads of America," has always been and remains a big attraction for lovers of sports, art, history, active rest, and family holidays from around the world. If you are planning an active trip to Indiana for the total eclipse with family or friends, you will have no problems finding something to do. Traveling through Indiana will inspire hope and bring you energy.

Indiana is a state in the Great Lakes region of the United States with a population of more than 6.5 million. The former French colony was admitted to the United States as the nineteenth state in 1816. Initially, the capital of Indiana was the city of Corydon. Indianapolis was founded and this rapidly growing city became the capital of the state in 1825. Today, Indianapolis is the largest city in Indiana.

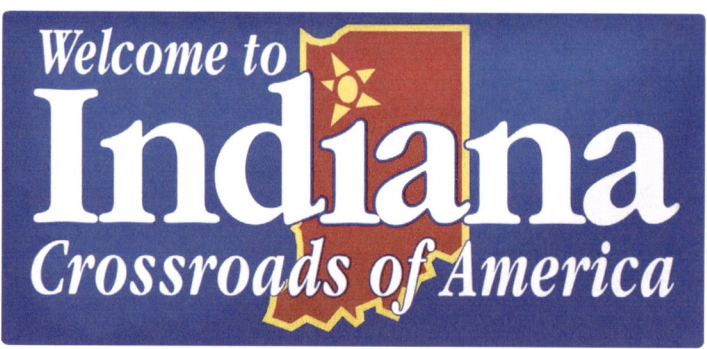

Indiana is located between the southern shore of Lake Michigan and the states of Ohio, Kentucky, and Illinois. This is a great place for fishing, playing sports, and having fun at numerous festivals. Indianapolis is the state's commercial and cultural center. You will need several days to explore this vibrant capital. Other major cities of the state are Fort Wayne, Evansville, South Bend, Carmel, Fishers, Hammond, and Gary. Any place within Indiana gives you great opportunities to have fun and view the eclipse on April 8, 2024.

Not many states can compete with Indiana in terms of the dynamics of life and leisure. This state offers a great variety of options for outdoor activities. Hiking and backpacking tours along the borders are very popular. People come here to take short walks through the

city streets or enjoy hiking along the long paths in the depths of the parks and natural areas like Brown County State Park, Mounds State Recreational Area, Green-Sullivan State Forest, and Hoosier National Forest.

Fishing lovers come to Indiana to spend time fishing on Lake Michigan or one of the numerous rivers. You can go cycling or horse riding through beautiful parks and reserves. This is a great opportunity to get acquainted with the sights and nature of the state.

Indianapolis is a true haven for motorsport and basketball lovers. The famous Indianapolis 500 race gathers hundreds of thousands of people in May. In August, you can attend the Brickyard 400 races. If you are a college sports fan, Indiana is a major basketball destination.

Indiana is ready to surprise art and history lovers with its museums, monuments, and galleries. While strolling through Indianapolis, visit the White River State Park, where the Indiana State Museum is located. A unique exhibition of Indiana's history is worth a stop. The museum also houses one of the four IMAX cinemas in Indiana.

Another venue worth visiting is the Indianapolis Museum of Art at Newfields. It is one of the nine oldest art museums in the United States. Tens of thousands of works are represented in the museum's collection, including works of African, American, Asian, and European artists. The collection includes paintings by neo-impressionists, Japanese paintings, Chinese ceramics and bronze, sculptures, and engravings by famous masters of America and Europe.

The Indiana War Memorial Plaza deserves special attention. It is dedicated to veterans of Indiana. The Soldiers and Sailors monument is built of limestone and bronze, decorated with bas-reliefs, and topped with a figure of the Statue of Liberty. The monument is included in the National Register of Historic Places of the United States.

Indiana is definitely a great place for family holidays. It is proud of the world's largest children's museum—The Children's Museum of Indianapolis. It houses about 120,000 exhibits. The collection includes the Broad Ripple Park carousel, dinosaurs, and a steam locomotive. The building is decorated with glass fireworks and a huge dinosaur. You'll need a day or two to explore the entire exhibition of this museum.

There is so much to explore and enjoy in Indiana before and after the total eclipse. Plan to spend some time visiting—you won't be disappointed. The people are friendly and more than willing to share their love of the state.

Hotels and Motels During the Eclipse

Once excitement of the total eclipse over Indiana spreads, rooms will become scarce. Many hotels in towns along the path of totality in western states sold out for a year or more during the 2017 total eclipse. Indiana is not alone in this challenge. Hotels all along the path of totality will sell out in anticipation of the 2024 total eclipse.

What does this mean for eclipse visitors? Lodging and room rentals in eclipse towns will be at a massive premium. Does that mean all hope is lost to find a place to stay? Not at all. But you will have to be creative. There will be few, if any, hotel rooms available in these eclipse cities by early 2024. Accommodations in the cities and towns along the path of the eclipse will be difficult to come by.

In summer 2017, the author searched on Hotels.com for rooms along the 2017 total eclipse path on the weekend of August 21 and found many major cities sold out. Once word of the 2024 eclipse spreads, room rates will increase and availability will drop.

Search for rooms farther away from the eclipse path. If you are willing to stay in cities outside the eclipse path, you will have better success at finding rooms. As the eclipse approaches, people will book rooms farther from the totality path. By early spring, rooms in cities near the total eclipse path may be unavailable. The effect of this event will be felt across Indiana and the rest of the United States.

Think regionally when looking for rooms. Be prepared to search far and wide during this major event. If a five-hour drive is manageable, your lodging options greatly expand, but it also increases your travel risk.

Internet Rentals

To find rooms to stay in towns along the eclipse path, try a web service such as Airbnb.com. Note that some people rent out rooms or homes illegally, against zoning regulations. Cities will feel the crunch of inquiries early due to others who experienced the 2017 eclipse.

If cities fully enforce zoning laws, authorities may prevent your weekend home rental. Online home rentals during the eclipse will be a target for rental scams. People from out of the area steal photos and descriptions, then post the home for rent. You send your check or wire money to a "rental agent" then show up to find you have been scammed. If the deal sounds strange or too good to be true, run away.

Camping

If you can book a campsite, do it as soon as you can. Do not wait. All areas in the national forests are first-come, first-served. Forest roads may be packed. Expect all areas to be swarming with people. Show up early to stake out your spot. Consider staying farther away and driving early on April 8.

Please respect private land too. Indiana folks don't take kindly to people overrunning their property without permission. In a big state with millions of residents, people are very protective, but they're friendly, too. You never know what you might be able to arrange with a smile and a bit of money.

This all said, there are plenty of camping opportunities throughout Indiana. You don't have to sleep exactly on the eclipse path. If you're ready to rough it, there are national forest camping options.

Government agencies will meet years in advance to talk about how to manage the influx of people. Every possible government agency will be working full time to enforce the various rules and regulations.

National Parks and Monuments

Finding a camping site at any state park, national park, or national monument along the eclipse path in Indiana will be challenging. To watch the eclipse from any location, you do not have to sleep in it. You just need to drive there in the morning.

Law enforcement will be present on the eclipse weekend. Hundreds of thousands of people are expected in the region. Parking may overflow. It will make parking lots and lines on Black Friday at the mall look uncrowded. For an event of this magnitude, find your location as early as possible.

The first sentence of the national parks mission statement is:

"The National Park Service preserves unimpaired the natural and cultural resources and values of the national park system for the enjoyment, education, and inspiration of this and future generations."

Roadside camping (sleeping in your car) is not allowed in national monuments or parks. Park facilities are only designed to handle so many people per day. Water, trash collection, and toilets can only withstand so much. If you notice trash on the ground, take a moment to throw it away. Protect your national park and help out. Rangers are diligent and hardworking but they can only do so much to manage the expected crowds.

National Forests and Wilderness

There are national forest options in Indiana. They all have camping opportunities. The forest service manages undeveloped and primitive campsites. Be sure to check for any fire restrictions. Check with individual agencies for last-minute information and regulations. The forest service requires proper food storage. Plan to purchase food and water before choosing your campsite. Below is a partial list of national forests along or near the total eclipse path:

Hoosier NF:
https://www.fs.usda.gov/hoosier

Backcountry service roads abound in Indiana. Maps for forests are available at local visitor centers and bookstores. This book's website has digital copies of some forest maps.

Printed national forest maps are large and detailed. They have illustrated road paths, connections, and other vital travel information not available on digital device maps. Viewing digital maps on your smartphone or mobile pad is difficult. If you plan to camp in the forest, a real paper map is a wise investment.

Camping in federal wilderness areas is also allowed. Those areas afford the ultimate backcountry experience. However, be aware that no vehicle travel is allowed in the specially designated areas. This ban includes: vehicles, bikes, hang gliders, and drones. You can travel only on foot or with pack animals.

Sleep in Your Car

Countless RVs, campers, trucks, cars, and motorcycles will flood Indiana. Sleeping in your car with friends is tolerable. Doing so with unadventurous spouses or children is another matter.

Do not be caught along the path of the total eclipse without some sort of plan, especially in the bigger cities of Indiana. The whole path of totality will fill with people on April 8.

Useful Local Webcams

Local webcams are handy to make last-minute travel decisions. Modern webcams are sensitive enough to show headlights at night. Use them to determine if there are issues before traveling out. Eclipse traffic will add to the morning commuter traffic.

There are smartphone applications which are useful to check webcams in many locations. Consult your device's app store for the latest updates. Whether you use an app or computer, an Internet search will reveal many handy webcams for your eclipse planning.

Weather

It's all about the weather during the eclipse. Nothing else will matter if the sky is cloudy. You can be nearly anywhere along the path in Indiana and catch a view of the event when traffic comes to a standstill. But if there's a cloud cover forecast, seriously reconsider your viewing location.

Travel early wherever you plan to go. Attempting to change locations an hour before the eclipse due to weather will likely cause you to miss the event. Indiana country roads can be narrow and slow. The number of vehicles will cause unexpected backups.

Modern Forecasts

Use a smartphone application to check the up-to-date weather. Wunderground is a good application and has relatively reliable forecasts for the region. The hourly forecast for the same day has been rather accurate for the last two years. The below discussion refers to features found in the Wunderground app. However, any application with detailed weather views will improve your eclipse forecasting skills.

Cloud Cover Forecast

The most useful forecast view is the visible and infrared cloud-coverage map. Avoid downloading this app the night before and trying to learn how to read it. Practice reading them at home. It's imperative to understand how to interpret the maps early.

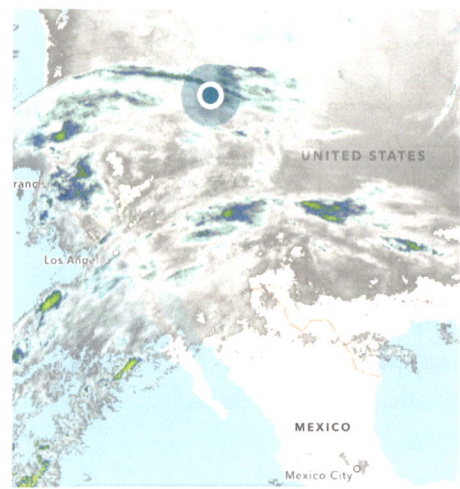

Infrared cloud map showing the worst case eclipse cloud cover. Courtesy of National Weather Service.

All cloud cover, night or day, will appear on an infrared map. Warm, low-altitude clouds are shown in white and gray. High-altitude cold clouds are displayed in shades of green, yellow, red, and purple. Anything other than a clear map spells eclipse-viewing problems.

To improve your weather guess, use the animated viewer of the cloud cover. It will give you a sense of cloud motion. You can discern whether clouds or rain are moving toward, away from, or circulating around your location.

Normal Indiana Weather Pattern

Due to the direction of the jet stream, most weather travels across the Pacific Ocean, through the western states, over the Rockies, and then into Indiana. On occasion, weather can approach from Canada or Mexico. Due to the nature of the storms from the Arctic, weather in Indiana can be unpredictable.

The common weather pattern in April is slightly warm in the afternoon and mildly cool in the evenings. Passing cold fronts in spring can bring unexpected cloud cover and rains.

Historically, Indiana tends to have moderate cloud cover during April. Prepare to make adjustments. If anything other than clear skies are predicted, drive to other parts of Indiana, Illinois, or Ohio.

Be aware of tornadoes in Indiana. Although the peak tornado season is June, there have been many recorded tornadoes in April. Pay attention to the weather forecast. If dangerous weather is predicted, your main concern should be safety rather than chasing an eclipse.

Consider that slow-moving clouds can obscure the sun for far longer than the four-minute duration of the totality. The time of totality is so short that you do not want to risk it. Missing it due to a single cloud will be a major disappointment.

Local Eclipse Weather Forecasts

Local town and city newspapers, radio, and television stations around Indiana will have a weekend edition with articles discussing the eclipse weather. However, conditions change unpredictably in Indiana. A three-day forecast for April may be incorrect.

Finding the Right Location to View Eclipse Effects

One of the peculiarities of total eclipses is that the entire show is not only in the sky. There are other unusual effects seen during the total eclipse that are worth looking for.

The first effect to watch for is the crescent moon shapes created from leaf shadows on the ground. They're best viewed on a sidewalk or asphalt. They can only be observed during the partial eclipse. The other effect that is worth watching for is the shadow bands or "snakes" as they're commonly called.

Shadow banding is seen right before and after the totality takes place. They're best observed on smooth, plain-colored surfaces. If you plan to be in the forest for the eclipse, you may struggle to see the bands but will likely see crescent shadows all around on the ground.

One of the supreme challenges with all of these effects is choosing what to watch. You can see the crescent shadows in the hour before and after the totality but shadow banding happens before or after totality. It is more difficult to look away from the eclipse than you think.

Road Closures and Traffic

Highways connecting various Indiana towns in the total eclipse path will be heavily impacted on the weekend before and day of the eclipse. As was found in the 2017 total eclipse, there is no way to predict which areas will be impacted.

Planning ahead is essential to give you the best opportunity to enjoy the eclipse without the nightmare of being stuck in traffic for hours on end. The traffic in Oregon and Idaho was stunning, so imagine what it will be like for Indiana.

Update yourself with the latest road report information from the Indiana road condition website:

http://pws.trafficwise.org/

It's imperative to plan early and have one if not more backup plans in case of difficult travel conditions. April weather is unpredictable and variable.

If you believe it's necessary to leave a town to watch the eclipse, do so the night before or extremely early in the morning. RVs are common, and trains of them crawl through popular areas.

Indiana Information

Cellular Phones

Cellular "cell" phone service in remote Indiana locations may be problematic. Most of the time there is good coverage along the main highways and interstates. However, even along major thoroughfares, there can be little or no coverage.

It's possible to find zones where text messages will send when phone calls are impossible. If you cannot make a phone call, the chance of having data coverage for web surfing or e-mail is low.

Please look up any information or communicate what you need before departing from the main roads around Indiana. Bureau of Land Management (BLM) areas sometimes have coverage. Planned to be self-contained. Plan for your cell phone not to connect.

You may find yourself out of cell service. With a large number of cell users in a concentrated area, coverage and data speed may collapse as well. Search on the phrase "cell phone coverage breathing".

Wilderness and Forest Safety

All Indiana forest and wilderness areas are full of wild animals. Although beautiful, wild animals can be dangerous. They can easily injure or kill people, as they are far more powerful than humans. Do not try to feed any wild animals, including squirrels, foxes, and chipmunks, as they can carry diseases. These suggestions apply to all public lands.

Feral Hogs

Introduced in the early twentieth century, hogs have become a major problem in Indiana. Although they tend to flee when encountered, hogs have been known to attack people. They can be aggressive and their tusks can inflict serious wounds. There have been instances of deaths, too. It is best to leave these animals alone if you encounter one.

Spiders

Although the chance of encountering a venomous spider is low, it is not uncommon to encounter them. The two dangerous spiders in the state are the black widow and brown recluse. Should you encouter either species, simply leave it alone. If you are bitten, seek immediate medical attention, as their toxin can be life-threatening.

Venomous Snakes

There are multiple species of venomous snakes in Indiana including the Copperhead, Cottonmouth, Eastern Massasauga Rattlesnake, and Timber Rattlesnake. Although these reptiles are not generally aggressive, they can strike when provoked or threatened. Of the approximately 8,000 people annually bitten by venomous snakes in the United States, ten to fifteen people die according to the U.S. Food and Drug Administration.

The best way to avoid rattlesnake encounters is to be mindful of your environment. Do not place your hands or feet in locations where you cannot clearly see the surroundings. Avoid heavy brush or tall weeds where snakes hide during the day. Step on a log or rock rather than over it, as a hidden snake might be on the other side. Rattlesnakes may not make any noise before striking.

Avoid handling all snakes. Should you be bitten, stay calm and call 911 or emergency dispatch as soon as possible. Transport the victim to the nearest medical facility immediately. Rapid professional treatment is the best way to manage rattlesnake bites. Refer to US Forest Service and professional medical texts for more information on managing rattlesnakes injuries.

Bears

The forests of Indiana are potentially home to black bears. Though they are listed rarely seen, they have been sighted in the state. Although they often appear docile, they can become aggressive if threatened. In the unlikely event of an attack, fight back against the bear. Use whatever you have at your disposal to defend yourself. Report all negative or aggressive bears to the local authorities.

If a bear hears you, it will usually vacate the area. Bear charges are often caused by unexpected and surprise encounters. Noise is the best defense to avoid surprising bears. Regularly clap, make noise, and talk loudly. The Indiana Department of Natural Resources website has more specific information on safety and food management in bear country at https://www.in.gov/dnr/fishwild/8500.htm.

It is recommended to stay one hundred yards (300 feet) away from all bears. They are exciting to see but need their space. Refer to current forest or park regulations for more safety information.

Mountain Lions

Though listed as extinct in the state, there have been recent reports of mountain lions in Indiana by the Indiana Department of Natural Resources. If you encounter a mountain lion, do not run. Keep calm, back away slowly, and maintain eye contact. Do all you can to appear larger. Stand upright, raise your arms, or hoist your jacket. Never bend over or crouch down. If attacked, fight back.

Eclipse Day Safety

1. Hydrate
Spring temperatures are usually mild to warm. The excitement of the event can distract you from managing hydration. Drink plenty of water. Consume more than you would at home.

2. Eye Safety time
Use certified eclipse safety glasses at all times when viewing the partial eclipse. Only remove the glasses when the totality happens. Give your eyes time to rest. They can dry out and become irritated. Bring FDA approved eye drops to keep your eyes moist.

3. Sun exposure
Facing at the sun for three hours can result in sunburns. Wear sunglasses and liberally apply sunscreen to avoid sunburns.

4. Eat well
Keep your energy up. Appetite loss is common when traveling. Maintain your normal eating schedule.

5. Prepare for temperature changes
Temperatures will drop rapidly during the eclipse and also once the sun sets. Bring appropriate clothing.

6. Talk with your doctor
If the humidity or heat bothers you talk with your doctor before traveling. Seek professional medical attention for serious symptoms.

18 ⊙ Indiana Total Eclipse Guide 2024

Total eclipse path across the United States (approximate).

Total eclipse path across Indiana (approximate).

All About Eclipses

How an Eclipse Happens

An eclipse occurs when one celestial body falls in line with another, thus obscuring the sun from view. This occurs much more often than you'd think, considering how many bodies there are in the solar system. For instance, there are over 150 moons in the solar system. On Earth, we have two primary celestial bodies: the sun and the moon. The entire solar system is constantly in motion, with planets orbiting the sun and moons orbiting the planets. These celestial bodies often come into alignment. When these alignments cause the sun to be blocked, it is called an eclipse.

For an eclipse to occur, the sun, Earth, and moon must be in alignment. There are two types of eclipses: solar and lunar. A solar eclipse occurs when the moon obscures the sun. A lunar eclipse occurs when the moon passes through Earth's shadow. Solar eclipses are much more common, as we experience an average of 240 solar eclipses a century compared to an average of 150 lunar eclipses. Despite this, we are more likely to see a lunar eclipse than a solar eclipse. This is due to the visibility of each.

For a solar eclipse to be visible, you have to be in the moon's shadow. The problem with viewing a total eclipse is that the moon casts a small shadow over the world at any given time. You have to be in

* ILLUSTRATION NOT TO SCALE

a precise location to view a total eclipse. The issue that arises is that most of these locations are inaccessible to most people. Though many would like to see a total solar eclipse, most aren't about to set sail for the middle of the Pacific Ocean. In fact, a solar eclipse is visible in the same place on the world on average every 375 years. This means that if you miss a solar eclipse above your hometown, you're not going to see another one unless you travel or move.

It's much easier to catch a glimpse of a lunar eclipse, even though they occur at a much lower frequency than their solar counterparts. A lunar eclipse darkens the moon for a few hours. This is different than a new moon when it faces away from the sun. During these eclipses, the moon fades and becomes nearly invisible.

Another result of a lunar eclipse is a blood moon. Earth's atmosphere bends a small amount of sunlight onto the moon turning it orange-red. The blood moon is caused by the dawn or dusk light being refracted onto the moon during an eclipse.

Lunar eclipses are much easier to see. Even when the moon is in the shadow of Earth, it's still visible throughout the world because of how much smaller it is than Earth.

Total vs. Partial Eclipse

What is the difference between a partial and total eclipse? A total eclipse of either the sun or the moon will occur only when the sun, Earth, and the moon are aligned in a perfectly straight line. This ensures that either the sun or the moon is partially or completely obscured.

In contrast, a partial eclipse occurs when the alignment of the three celestial bodies is not in a perfectly straight line. These types of eclipses usually result in only a part of either the sun or the moon being obscured. This is often what led to ancient civilizations believing that some form of magical beast or deity was eating the sun or the moon. It appears as though something has taken a bite out of either the sun or the moon during a partial eclipse.

Total eclipses, rarer than partial eclipses, still occur quite often. It's more difficult for people to be in a position to experience such an event firsthand. Total solar eclipses can only be viewed from a small portion of the world that falls into the darkest part of the moon's shadow. Often this happens in the middle of the ocean.

THE MOON'S SHADOW

The moon's shadow is divided into two parts: the umbra and the penumbra. The former is much smaller than the latter, as the umbra is the innermost and darkest part of the shadow. The umbra is thus the central point of the moon's shadow, meaning that it is extremely small in comparison to the entire shadow. For a total solar eclipse to be visible, you need to be directly beneath the umbra of the moon's shadow. This is because that is the only point at which the moon completely blocks the view of the sun.

In contrast, the penumbra is the region of the moon's shadow in which only a portion of the light cast by the sun is obscured. When

Total eclipse shadow 2016 as seen from 1 million miles on the Deep Space Climate Observatory satellite. Courtesy of NASA.

standing in the penumbra, you are viewing the eclipse at an angle. In the penumbra, the moon does not completely block the sun from view. This means that while the event is a total solar eclipse, you'll only see a partial eclipse. The umbra for the April 8 eclipse is over one hundred miles wide. The penumbra will cover much of the United States.

To provide some context, one total solar eclipse we experienced occurred on March 9, 2016, and was visible as a partial eclipse across most of the Pacific Ocean, parts of Asia, and Australia. However, the only place in the world to view this total solar eclipse was in a few parts of Indonesia.

Due to the varied locations and the brief periods for which they're visible, it's difficult to see each and every eclipse that occurs. The umbra of the moon is such a small fraction of the entire shadow and the majority of our planet is comprised of water. Thus, the rarity of being able to view a total solar eclipse increases significantly because it's likely that the umbra will fall over some part of the ocean rather than a populated landmass. There are not total or annular eclipses every month because the moon's orbit is 5.1° off the ecliptic plane of the Earth and sun.

Eclipses Throughout History

Ancient peoples believed eclipses were from the wrath of angry gods, portents of doom and misfortune, or wars between celestial beings. Eclipses have played many roles in cultures, creating myths since the dawn of time. Both solar and lunar eclipses affected societies worldwide. Inspiring fear, curiosity, and the creation of legends, eclipses have cast a long shadow in the collective unconscious of humanity throughout history.

Early Myth & Astronomy

Documented observations of solar eclipses have been found as far back in history as ancient Egyptian and Chinese records. Timekeeping was important to ancient Chinese cultures. Astronomical

observations were an integral factor in the Chinese calendar. The first observation of a solar eclipse is found in Chinese records from over 4,000 years ago. Evidence suggests that ancient Egyptian observations may predate those archaic writings.

Many ancient societies, including Roman, Greek and Chinese civilizations, were able to infer and foresee solar eclipses from astronomical data. The sudden and unpredictable nature of solar eclipses had a stressful and intimidating effect on many societies that lacked the scientific insight to accurately predict astronomical events. Relying on the sun for their agricultural livelihood, those societies interpreted solar eclipses as world-threatening disasters.

In ancient Vietnam, solar eclipses were explained as a giant frog eating the sun. The peasantry of ancient Greece believed that an eclipse was the sign of a furious godhead, presenting an omen of wrathful retribution in the form of natural disasters. Other cultures were less speculative in their investigations. The Chinese Song Dynasty scientist Shen Kuo proved the spherical nature of the Earth and heavenly bodies through scientific insight gained by the study of eclipses.

THE ECLIPSE IN NATIVE AMERICAN MYTHOLOGY

Eclipses have played a significant role in the history of the United States. Before Europeans settled in the Americas, solar eclipses were important astronomical events to Native American cultures. In most native cultures, an eclipse was a particularly bad omen. Both the sun and the moon were regarded as sacred. Viewing an eclipse, or even being outside for the duration of the event, was considered highly taboo by the Navajo culture. During an eclipse, men and women would simply avert their eyes from the sky, acting as though it was not happening.

The Choctaw people had a unique story to explain solar eclipses. Considering the event as the mischievous actions of a black squirrel and its attempt to eat the sun, the Choctaw people would do their best to scare away the cosmic squirrel by making as much noise as

possible until the end of the event, at which point cognitive bias would cause them to believe they'd once again averted disaster on an interplanetary scale.

Contemporary American Solar Phenomena

The investigation of solar phenomena in twentieth-century American history had a similarly profound effect on the people of the United States. A total solar eclipse occurring on the sixteenth of June, 1806, engulfed the entire country. It started near modern-day Arizona. It passed across the Midwest, over Ohio, Pennsylvania, New York, Massachusetts, and Connecticut. The 1806 total eclipse was notable for being one of the first publicly advertised solar events. The public was informed beforehand of the astronomical curiosity through a pamphlet written by Andrew Newell entitled *Darkness at Noon, or the Great Solar Eclipse*.

This pamphlet described local circumstances and went into great detail explaining the true nature of the phenomenon, dispelling myth and superstition, and even giving questionable advice on the best methods of viewing the sun during the event. Replete with a short historical record of eclipses through the ages, the *Darkness at Noon* pamphlet is one of the first examples of an attempt to capitalize on the mysterious nature of solar eclipses.

Another notable American solar eclipse occurred on June 8, 1918. Passing over the United States from Washington to Florida, the eclipse was accurately predicted by the U.S. Naval Observatory and heavily documented in the newspapers of the day. Howard Russell Butler, painter and founder of the American Fine Arts Society, painted the eclipse from the U.S. Naval Observatory, immortalizing the event in *The Oregon Eclipse*.

Four more total solar eclipses occurred over the United States in the years 1923, 1925, 1932, and 1954, with another occurring in 1959. The October 2, 1959, solar eclipse began over Boston, Massachusetts. It was a sunrise event that was unviewable from the ground level. Eminent astronomer Jay Pasachoff attributed this event to sparking his interest in the study of astronomy. Studying under Professor Donald Menzel of Williams College, Pasachoff was able to view the event from an airline hired by his professor.

To this day, many myths surround the eclipse. In India, some local customs require fasting. In eastern Africa, eclipses are seen as a danger to pregnant women and young children. Despite the mystery and legend associated with unique and rare astronomical events, eclipses continue to be awe-inspiring. Even in the modern day, eclipses draw out reverential respect for the inexorable passing of celestial bodies. They are a reminder of the intimate relationship between the denizens of Earth and the universe at large.

Present Day Eclipses

The year 2017 brought the world's most-watched total eclipse in history on August 21, when a total solar eclipse crossed the United States. An annular eclipse, a "ring of fire," will pass over the United States in 2023 from Oregon to Texas. Though impressive, it will not

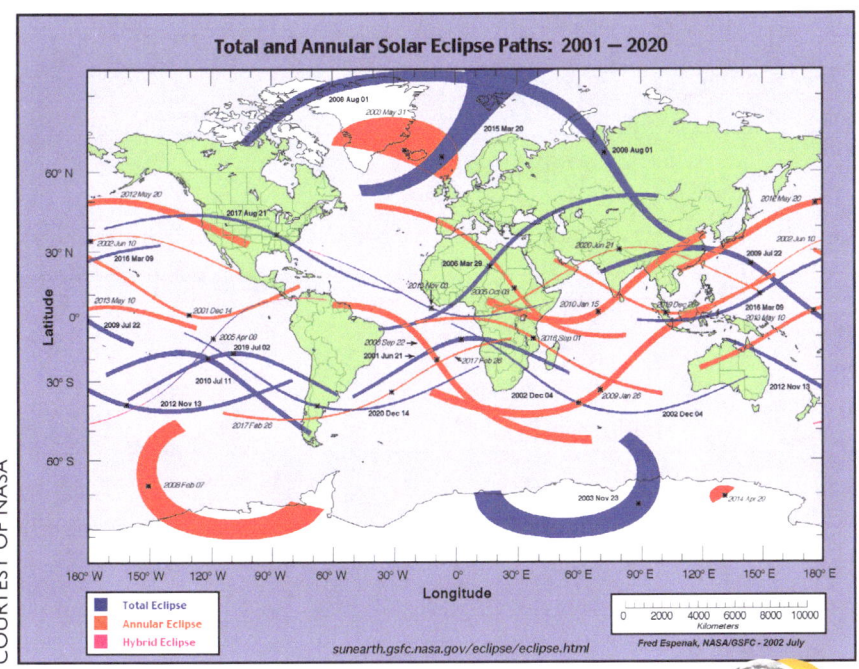

compare to the 2024 total eclipse. There is little in nature that equals the spectacle of the sun's corona and seeing stars in the day.

There will be multiple partial, annular, or hybrid eclipses across the world before the 2024 total eclipse. However many are in remote, inaccessible, or potentially dangerous locations on the globe. In 2019 and 2020, Chile and Argentina will experience total eclipses. The next total eclipse after that will occur over Antarctica in 2021. An extremely rare hybrid eclipse will happen in 2023 over the Indian Ocean, Australia, and Indonesia.

The next total solar eclipse viewable from the United States will occur on April 8, 2024. It will be visible in fifteen states: Texas, Oklahoma, Arkansas, Missouri, Tennessee, Kentucky, Illinois, Indiana, Ohio, Pennsylvania, Michigan, New York, Vermont, New Hampshire, and Maine.

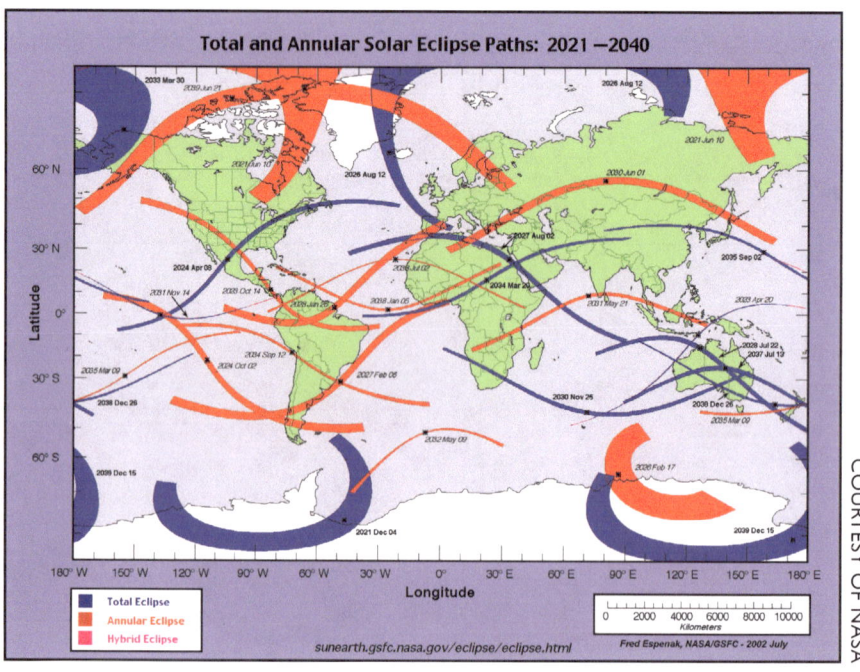

COURTESY OF NASA

Viewing and Photographing the Eclipse

AT-HOME PINHOLE METHOD

Use the pinhole method to view the eclipse safely. It costs little but is the safest technique there is. Take a stiff piece of single-layer cardboard and punch a clean pinhole. Let the sun shine through the pinhole onto another piece of cardboard. That's it!

Never look at the sun through the pinhole. Your back should be toward the sun to protect your eyes. To brighten the image, simply move the back piece of cardboard closer to the pinhole. To see it larger, move the back cardboard farther away. Do not make the pinhole larger. It will only distort the crescent sun.

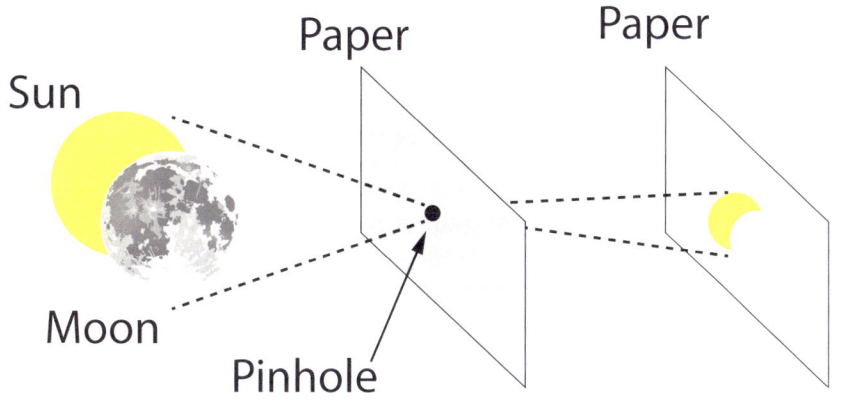

WELDING GOGGLES

Welding goggles that have a rating of fourteen or higher are another useful eclipse viewing tool. The goggles can be used to view the solar eclipse directly. Do not use the goggles to look through binoculars or telescopes, as the goggles could potentially shatter due to intense direct heat. Avoid long periods of gazing with the goggles. Look away every so often. Give your eyes a break.

SOLAR FILTERS FOR TELESCOPES

The ONLY safe way to view solar eclipses using telescopes or binoculars is to use solar filters. The filters are coated with metal to diminish the full intensity of the sun. Although the filters can be expensive, it is better to purchase a quality filter rather than an inexpensive one that could shatter or melt from the heat.

The filters attach to the front of the telescope for easy viewing. Remember to give your telescope cooling breaks. Rapid heating can damage your equipment with or without filters attached.

Watch Out for Unsafe Filters

There are several myths surrounding solar filters for eclipse viewing. In order for filters to be safe, they must be specially designed for looking at a solar eclipse. The following are all unsafe for eclipse viewing and can lead to retinal damage: developed colored or chromogenic film, black-and-white negatives such as X-rays, CDs with aluminum, smoked glass, floppy disk covers, black-and-white film with no silver, sunglasses, or polarizing films.

Watch Out for Unsafe Eclipse Glasses

During the 2017 total eclipse, several vendors sold eclipse glasses that were not safe for viewing the sun. Although they were marketed as safe and were even marked with the ISO 12312-2 certification, they did not block eye-damaging visible, infrared, and ultraviolet light. Check the American Astronomical Society's website (eclipse.aas.org) for a list of reputable eclipse glasses vendors.

Viewing with Binoculars

When viewing the eclipse with binoculars, it is important to use solar filters on both lenses until totality. Only then is it safe to remove the filter. As the sun becomes visible after totality, replace the filters for safe viewing. Protect your pupils. Remember to give your binoculars a cool-down break between viewings. They can overheat rapidly from being pointed directly at the sun even with filters attached.

Planning Ahead

There are many things to keep in mind when viewing a total eclipse. It is important to plan ahead to get the most out of this extraordinary experience.

Understanding Sun Position

All compass bearings in this book are true north. All compasses point to Earth's magnetic north. The difference between these two measurements is called magnetic declination. The magnetic declination for Indiana is:

4° 59' W ± 0° 22' (for Indianapolis in 2024)

Adjust the declination from the azimuth bearing as given in the text, and set your compass to that direction.

If you purchase a compass with a built-in declination adjustment, you can change the setting once and eliminate the calculations. The Suunto M-3G compass has this correction. A compass with a sighting mirror or wire will help you make a more accurate azimuth sighting.

The Suunto M-3G also has an inclinometer. This allows you to measure the elevation of any object above the horizon. Use this to figure out how high the sun will be above your position.

You can also use a smartphone inclinometer and compass for this purpose. Make sure to calibrate your smartphone's compass before every use, otherwise it might indicate the wrong bearing. Set the smartphone compass for true north to match the book. Understand the compass prior to April 8. There will be little time to guess or search on Google. Smartphone and GPS compasses are "sticky." Their compasses don't swing as freely as a magnetic compass does.

The author has used his magnetic compass for azimuth measurements and a smartphone to measure elevation. Combining these two tools will allow you to make the best sightings possible.

Outdoor sporting goods stores in most towns and cities carry compasses. Purchase and practice with a good compass in your hometown well before the event. Take the time to learn how to use it before the day of the eclipse. You do not want to struggle with orienteering basics under pressure.

Sun Azimuth

Azimuth is the compass angle along the horizon, with 0º corresponding to north, and increasing in a clockwise direction. 90º is east, 180º is south, and 270º is west.

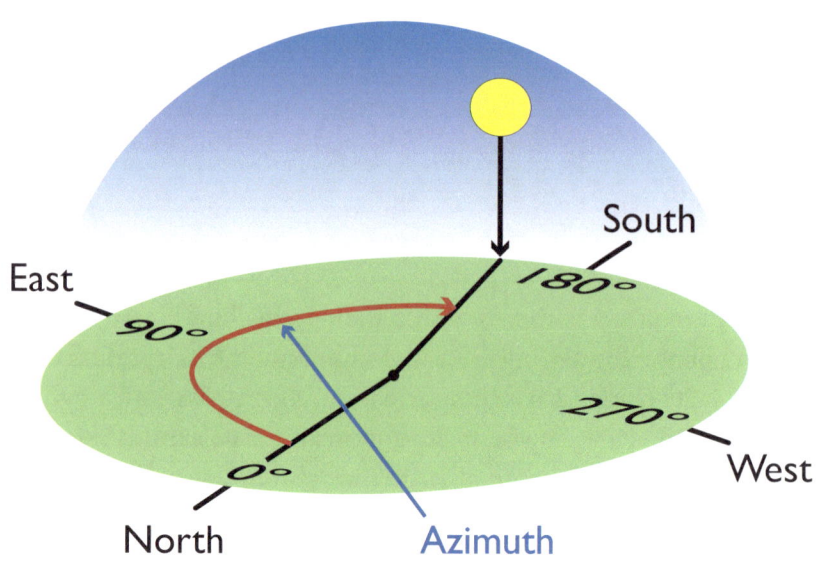

Sun Elevation

Altitude is the sun's angle up from the horizon. A 0º altitude means exactly on the horizon and 90º means "straight up."

Using the sun azimuth and elevation data, you can predict the position of the sun at any given time. Positions given in this book coincide with the time of eclipse totality unless otherwise noted.

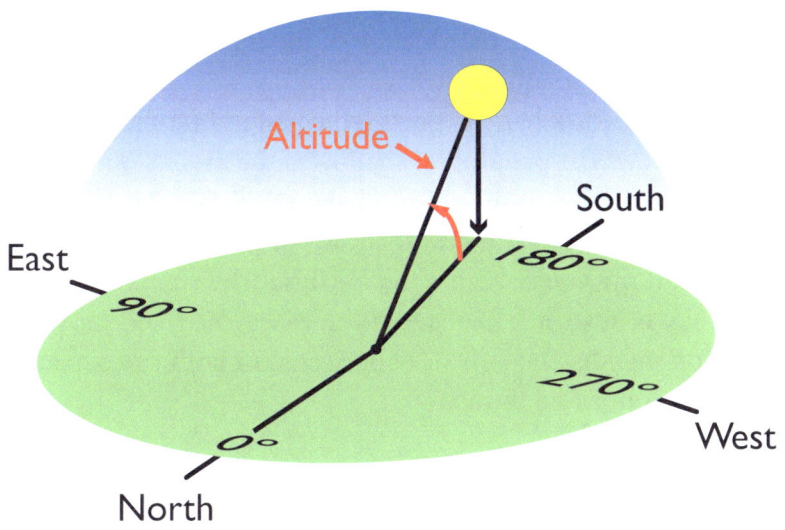

Eclipse Data for Select Indiana Locations

LOCATION	TOTALITY START (EDT)	ALTITUDE	AZIMUTH
BEDFORD	3:04:41PM	54°	214°
BLUFFTON	3:08:52PM	51°	216°
GREENCASTLE	3:05:04PM	53°	213°
INDIANAPOLIS	3:05:58PM	53°	214°
JASPER	3:03:48PM	54°	214°
MUNCIE	3:07:29PM	52°	215°

Eclipse Photography

Photographing an eclipse is an exciting challenge, as the moon's shadow moves near 1,600MPH. There is an element of danger and the pressure of time. Looking at the unfiltered sun through a camera can permanently damage your vision and your camera. If you are unsure, just enjoy the eclipse with specially designed eclipse glasses. Keep a solar filter on your lens during the eclipse and remove for the duration of totality!

Partial Vs. Total Solar Eclipse

To successfully and safely photograph a partial and total eclipse, it is important to understand the difference between the two. A solar eclipse occurs when the moon is positioned between the sun and Earth. The region where the shadow of the moon falls upon Earth's surface is where a solar eclipse is visible.

The moon's shadow has two parts—the penumbral shadow and the umbral shadow. The penumbral shadow is the moon's outer shadow where partial solar eclipses can be observed. Total solar eclipses can only be seen within the umbral shadow, the moon's inner shadow.

You cannot say you've seen a total eclipse when all you saw was a partial solar eclipse. It is like saying you've watched a concert, but in reality, you only listened outside the arena. In both cases, you have missed the drama and the action.

Photographing A Partial And Total Solar Eclipse

Aside from the region where the outer shadow of the moon is cast, a partial solar eclipse is also visible before a total solar eclipse within

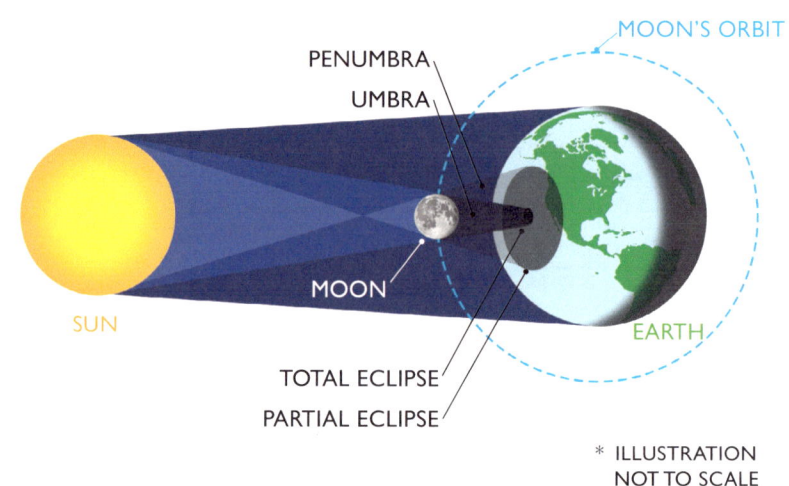

the inner shadow region. In both cases, it is imperative to use a solar filter on the lens for both photography and safety reasons. This is the only difference between taking a partial eclipse and a total eclipse photograph of the sun.

To photograph a total solar eclipse, you must be within the Path of Totality, the surface of the Earth within the moon's umbral shadow.

The Challenge

A total solar eclipse only lasts for a couple of minutes. It is brief, but the scenario it brings is unforgettable. Seeing the radiant sun slowly being covered by darkness gives the spectator a high level of anticipation and indescribable excitement. Once the moon completely covers the sun's radiance, the corona is finally visible. In the darkness, the sun's corona shines, capturing the crowd's full attention. Watching this phenomenon is a breathtaking experience.

Amidst all the noise, cheering, and excitement, you have no more than a few minutes to take a perfect photograph. The key to this is planning. You need to plan, practice, and perfect what you will do when the big moment arrives because there is no replay. The pressure is enormous. You only have a short time to capture the totality and the sun's corona using different exposures.

Plan, Practice, Perfect

It is important to practice photographing before the actual phenomenon arrives. Test your chosen imaging setup for flaws. Rehearse over and over until your body remembers what you will do from the moment you arrive at your chosen spot to the moment you pack up and leave the area.

You will discover potential problems regarding vibrations and focus that you can address immediately. This minimizes the variables that might affect your photographs at the most critical moment.

It's common for experienced eclipse chasers to lose track of what they plan to do. Write down what you expect to do. Practice it time and again. Play annoying, distracting music while you practice. Try photographing in the worst weather possible. Do anything you can to practice under pressure. Eclipse day is not the time to practice.

Once the sun is completely covered, don't just take photographs. Capture the experience and the image of the total solar eclipse in your mind as well. Set up cameras around you to record not just the total solar eclipse but also the excitement and reaction of the crowd.

Eclipse Photography Gear

What do you need to photograph the total eclipse? There are only a few pieces of equipment that you'll need. Preparing to photograph an eclipse successfully takes time. Not only do you have to be skilled and have the right gear, you have to be in the correct place.

Basic Eclipse Photography Equipment

- Solar viewing glasses (verify authenticity)
- Lens solar filter
- Minimum 300mm lens
- Stable tripod that can be tilted to 60° vertical
- High-resolution DSLR
- Spare batteries for everything
- Secondary camera to photograph people, the horizon, etc.
- Remote cable or wireless release

Additional Items

- Video camera
- Video camera tripod
- Quality pair of binoculars
- Solar filters for each binocular lens
- Photo editing software

Equipment to Prepare Before the Big Day

A. Solar viewing glasses

You need a pair of solar viewing glasses as the eclipse approaches.

B. Solar Filter

Partial and total eclipse photography is different from normal photography. Even if only 1% of the sun's surface is visible, it is still approximately 10,000 times brighter than the moon. Before totality, use a solar filter on your lens. Do not look at the sun with your eyes. It can cause irreparable damage to your retinas.

DO NOT leave your camera pointed at the sun without a solar filter attached. The sun will melt the inside of your camera. Think of a magnifying glass used to torch ants and multiply that by one hundred.

C. Lens

To capture the corona's majesty, you need to use a telescope or a telephoto lens. The best focal length, which will give you a large image of the sun's disk, is 400mm and above. You don't want to waste all your efforts by bringing home a small dot where the black disk and majestic corona are supposed to be.

D. Tripod

Bring a stable enough tripod to support your camera properly to avoid unsteady shots and repeated adjustments. Either will ruin your photos. It also needs to be portable in case you need to change locations for a better shot. *Shut off camera stabilization on a tripod!*

E. Camera

You need to remember to set your camera to its highest resolution to capture all the details. Set your camera to:

- 14-bit RAW is ideal, otherwise
- JPG, Fine compression, Maximum resolution

Bracket your exposures. Shoot at various shutter speeds to capture different brightnesses in the corona. Note that stopping your lens all the way down may not result in the sharpest images.

Choose the lowest possible ISO for the best quality while maintaining a high shutter speed to prevent blurred shots. Set your camera to manual. Do not use AUTO ISO. Your camera will be fooled. The night before, test the focus position of your lens using a bright star or the moon.

Constantly double-check your focus. Be paranoid about this. You can deal with a grainy picture. No amount of Photoshop will fix a blurry, out-of-focus picture.

F. Batteries

Remember to bring fresh batteries! Make sure that you have enough power to capture the most important moments. Swap in fresh batteries thirty minutes before totality.

G. Remote release

Use a wired or wireless remote release to fire the camera's shutter. This will reduce the amount of camera vibration.

H. Video Camera

Run a video camera of yourself. Capture all the things you say and do during the totality. You'll be amazed at your reaction.

I. Photo editing software

You will need quality photo editing software to process your eclipse images. Adobe Lightroom and Photoshop are excellent programs to extract the most out of your images. Become well versed in how to use them at least a month before the eclipse.

J. Smartphone applications

The following smartphone applications will aid in your photography planning: Wunderground, Skyview, Photographer's Ephemeris, Sunrise and Sunset Calculator, SunCalc, and Sun Surveyor among others.

CAMERA PHONES

Smartphone cameras are useful for many things but not eclipse photography. An iPhone 6 camera has a 63° horizontal field of view and is 3264 pixels across. If you attempt to photograph the eclipse, the sun will be a measly 30-40 pixels wide depending on the phone. Digital pinch zoom won't help here. If you want *National Geographic* images, you'll need a serious camera and lens, far beyond any smartphone.

Consider instead using a smartphone to run a time-lapse of the entire event. The sun will be minuscule when shot on a smartphone. Think of something else exciting and interesting do to with it. Purchase a Gorilla Pod, inexpensive tripod, or selfie stick and mount the smartphone somewhere unique.

Also, partial and total eclipse light is strange and ethereal. Consider using that light to take unique pictures of things and people. It's rare and you may have something no one else does.

Focal Length & the Size of Sun

The size of the sun in a photo depends on the lens focal length. A 300mm lens is the recommended minimum on a full-frame (FF) DSLR. Lenses up to this size are relatively inexpensive. For more magnification, use an APS-C (crop) size sensor. Cameras with these sensors provide an advantage by capturing a larger sun.

For the same focal length, an APS-C sensor will provide a greater apparent magnification of any object. As a consequence, a shorter, less expensive lens can be used to capture the same size sun.

The below figure shows the size of the sun on a camera sensor at various focal lengths. As can be seen with the 200mm lens, the sun is quite small. On a full-frame camera at 200mm, the sun will be 371 pixels wide on a Nikon D810, a 36-megapixel body. A lower resolution FF camera will result in an even smaller sun.

Printing a 24-inch image shot on a Nikon D810 with a 200mm lens at a standard 300 pixels per inch results in a small sun. On this size paper, the sun will be a miserly 1.25 inches wide!

Photographing the eclipse with a lens shorter than 300mm will leave you with little to work with. Using a 400mm lens and printing a 24-inch print will result in a 2.5-inch-wide sun. For as massive as the sun is, it is a challenge to take a large photograph of the sun. The sun will appear to move fast with a 500mm lens, too. Plan to adjust.

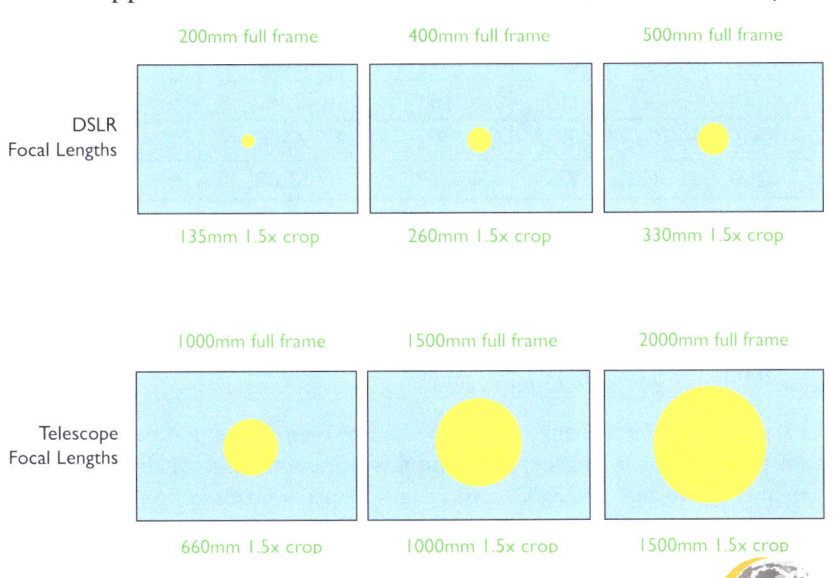

	200mm full frame	400mm full frame	500mm full frame
DSLR Focal Lengths			
	135mm 1.5x crop	260mm 1.5x crop	330mm 1.5x crop
	1000mm full frame	1500mm full frame	2000mm full frame
Telescope Focal Lengths			
	660mm 1.5x crop	1000mm 1.5x crop	1500mm 1.5x crop

FOCAL LENGTH	FOV FULL FRAME	FF VERT. ANGLE	% OF FF	SUN PIXEL SIZE
14	104° X 81°	81°	0.7%	32.1
20	84° X 62°	62°	0.9%	41.9
28	65° X 46°	46°	1.2%	56.5
35	54° X 38°	38°	1.4%	68.5
50	40° X 27°	27°	2.0%	96.4
105	19° X 13°	13°	4.1%	200.2
200	10° X 7°	7°	7.6%	371.9
400	5° X 3.4°	3.4°	15.6%	765.6
500	4° X 2.7°	2.7°	19.6%	964.2
1000	2° X 1.3°	1.3°	40.8%	2002.5
1500	1.4° X 0.9°	0.9°	58.9%	2892.6
2000	1° X 0.68°	0.68°	77.9%	3828.4

Chart 1: Full-frame camera field of view. The 3rd column is the vertical field of view in degrees. Column 4 is the percentage of the total sensor height that the sun covers. Column 5 is how many pixels wide the sun will be on a 36MP Nikon D810. (Values are estimates)

FOCAL LENGTH	FOV CROP	CROP VERT DEG	% OF CROP	SUN PIXEL SIZE
14	80° X 58°	58°	0.9%	33.9
20	61° X 43°	43°	1.2%	45.8
28	45° X 31°	31°	1.7%	63.5
35	37° X 25°	25°	2.1%	78.7
50	26° X 18°	18°	2.9%	109.3
105	13° X 8°	8°	6.6%	245.9
200	6.7° X 4.5°	4.5°	11.8%	437.2
400	3.4° X 2°	2°	26.5%	983.7
500	2.7° X 1.8	1.8°	29.4%	1093.0
1000	1.3° X 0.9°	0.9°	58.9%	2186.0
1500	0.9° X 0.6°	0.6°	88.3%	3278.9
2000	0.6° X 0.45°	0.5°	117.8%	4371.9

Chart 2: APS-C Crop sensor camera field of view. The 3rd column is the vertical field of view in degrees. Column 4 is the percentage of the total sensor height that the sun covers. Column 5 is how many pixels wide the sun will be on a 12mp Nikon D300s. (Values are estimates)

The big challenge is the cost of the lens. Lenses longer than 300mm are expensive. They also require heavier tripods and specialized tripod heads. The 70-300mm lenses from Nikon, Canon, Tamron, and others are relatively affordable options. It is worth spending time at a local camera shop to try different lenses. Long focal-length lenses are a significant investment, especially for a single event.

To achieve a large eclipse image, you will need a long focal-length lens, ideally at least 400mm. A standard 70-300mm lens set to 300mm will show a small sun. At 500mm, the sun image becomes larger and covers more of the sensor area. The corona will take up a significant portion of the frame. By 1000mm, the corona will exceed the capture area on a full-frame sensor. See the picture in this chapter for sun size simulations for different focal lengths.

Suggested Exposures

To photograph the partial eclipse, the camera must have a solar filter attached. If not, the intense light from the sun may damage (fry) the inside of your camera. This has happened to the author. The exposure depends on the density (darkness) of the solar filter used.

As a starting point, set the camera to ISO 100, f/8, and with the solar filter on, try an exposure of 1/2000. Make adjustments based on the filter used, histogram, and highlight warning.

Turn on the highlight warning in your camera. This feature is commonly called "blinkies." This warning will help you detect if the image is overexposed or not.

Once the Baily's Beads, prominences, and corona become visible, there will only be a few minutes to take bracketed shots. It will take at least eleven shots to capture the various areas of the sun's corona and stars. The brightness varies considerably. No commercially available camera can capture the incredible dynamic range of the different portions of the delicate corona. This requires taking multiple photographs and digitally combining them afterward.

During totality, try these exposure times at ISO 100 and f/8: 1/4000, 1/2000, 1/1000, 1/250, 1/60, 1/30, 1/15, 1/4, 1/2, 1 sec, and 4 sec.

Disable camera/lens stabilization on a tripod!

Photography Time

Set the camera to full-stop adjustments. It will reduce the time spent fiddling. As an example, the author tried the above shot sequence, adjusting the shutter speed as fast as possible.

It took thirty-three seconds to shoot the above 11 shots using 1/3-stop increments. This was without adjusting composition, focus, or anything else but the shutter speed. When the camera was set to full stop increments, it only took twenty-two seconds to step through the same shutter speed sequence. Use a remote release to reduce camera shake.

Assuming the totality lasts less than two minutes, only four shot sequences could be made using 1/3-stop increments. Yet six shot sequences could be made when the camera was set to full stop steps. Zero time was spent looking at the back LCD to analyze highlights and the histogram.

Now add in the bare minimum time to check the highlight warning. It took sixty-three seconds to shoot and check each image using full stops. And that was without changing the composition to allow for sun movement, bumping the tripod, etc. Looking at the LCD ("chimping") consumed **half** of the totality time.

This test was done in the comfort of home under no pressure. In real world conditions, it may be possible to successfully shoot only one sequence. If you plan to capture the entire dynamic range of the totality, you must practice the sequence until you have it down cold. If you normally fumble with your camera, do not underestimate the difficulty, frustration, and stress of total eclipse photography.

Most importantly, trying to shoot this sequence allowed for zero time to simply look at the totality to enjoy the spectacle.

Avoid Last Minute Purchases

You should purchase whatever you think you'll need to photograph the eclipse early. This event will be nothing short of massive. Remember the hot toy of the year? Multiply that frenzy by a thousand. Everyone will want to try to capture their own photo.

Do not wait until the last few weeks before the eclipse to purchase cameras, lenses, filters, tripods, viewing glasses, and associated material. Consider that the totality of the eclipse will streak across

America. Everyone who wants to photograph the eclipse will order at the same time. If you wait until too late to buy what you need, it's conceivable that solar filters to create a total eclipse photo will be sold out in the United States. All filters sold out during the 2017 total eclipse. Whether this happens or not, do not wait to make your purchases. It may be too late.

Practice

You will need to practice with your equipment. Things may go wrong that you don't anticipate. If you've never photographed a partial or total eclipse, taking quality shots is more difficult than you think. Practice shooting the sequence with a midday sun. This will tell you if you have your exposures and timing correct. Figure out what you need well in advance.

Practice photographing the full moon and stars at night. Capture the moon in full daylight to learn how your camera reacts. Astrophotography is challenging and requires practice.

The August 21, 2017, eclipse as seen in Jackson, WY, shot with a Nikon D800 with an 80-400mm lens set to 340mm. The sun is 644 pixels wide on the 7360x4912 image.

This image is shown straight out of the camera without modification. Even with a high-quality camera and lens, photographing an eclipse is challenging.

42 ☉ Indiana Total Eclipse Guide 2024

— Sun's path from sunrise   Total eclipse position

The eclipse will follow this approximate path on the afternoon of April 8, 2024. Image of the Indiana War Memorial Plaza, downtown Indianapolis, IN.

Note that this image is a simulation and approximation the sun's path and where the total eclipse may appear from one perspective. Refer to the eclipse position data for a more accurate location.

LOCATIONS

☉ is the symbol for the sun and first appeared in Europe during the Renaissance.
☾ is the ancient symbol for the moon.

Viewing Locations Around Indiana

Tens of thousands of people will travel to and around Indiana to view the total eclipse. There are few obstructions and there is a vast amount of space to view the total eclipse from.

If the weather is questionable, seek out a new location as soon as possible. If you wait until the hour before the eclipse, you may find yourself stuck in traffic, as others will be looking for a viewing location. Be safe on the roadways, as drivers may be distracted.

This section contains popular, alternative, and little-known locations to watch the eclipse. As long as there are no clouds or smoke from fires, the partial eclipse will be viewable from anywhere in the state.

Suggested Total Eclipse View Points

Towns and Cities

- Anderson
- Bedford
- Bloomington
- Bluffton
- Connersville
- Columbus
- Evansville
- Greencastle
- Indianapolis
- Jasper
- Marion
- Muncie
- Richmond
- Portland
- Seymour
- Terre Haute
- Washington

Unique Locations

- Brown County State Park
- Green-Sullivan State Forest
- Hoosier National Forest
- Mounds State Park

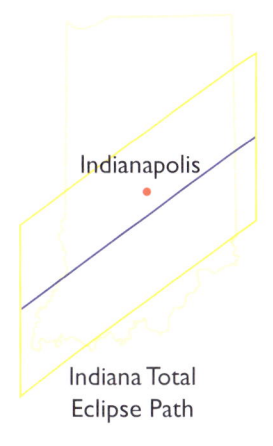

Anderson

Elevation:	879 feet
Population:	55,067
Main road/hwy:	I-69

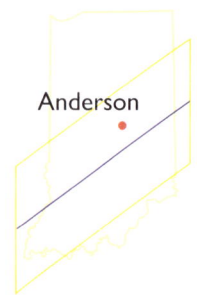

Overview

Named after Chief William Adam Anderson, the city finds mention in the novel *The Man with the Iron Heart* and is a must visit. The city provides a friendly environment for trading activities due to the availability of good transport networks like roads and railways. It is also home to Anderson University, a private Christian liberal arts college. There are several historical sites such as Saint Mary's Catholic Church, Anderson Fine Arts Center, and Trinity Episcopal Church, which tourists love to visit.

Getting There

Drive from Indianapolis northeast on I-70 E, merge onto I-465 N, and continue on I-69 N. Take the Dr. Martin Luther King Jr. Blvd. exit and drive north into Anderson.

Totality Duration

3 minutes 39 seconds

Notes

Visit the city's official website at https://www.cityofanderson.com/ for updated eclipse information.

Event	Time (EDT)	Altitude	Azimuth
Sunrise	7:14:00AM	0°	79°
Eclipse Start	1:51:37PM	57°	183°
Totality Start	3:07:02PM	52°	215°
Totality End	3:10:41PM	52°	216°
Eclipse End	4:23:50PM	41°	238°
Sunset	8:14:00PM	0°	280°

Bedford

Elevation: 686 feet
Population: 13,296
Main road/hwy: US 50

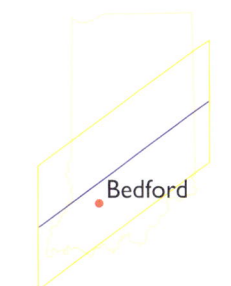

Overview

Known as the limestone capital of the world, the city lies in Southern Indiana and named so because of the stone terrain. The city has an 800-foot limestone replica of the Great Wall of China and also houses the Bedford Little Theatre, the Mitchell Opera House, and the Lawrence County Museum of History. While the Carousel Winery is a great destination for wine tasters, nature lovers will love to visit the Spring Mill State Park, Bluespring Caverns Park, and the Hidden Falls Camp.

Getting There

Drive south from Indianapolis on IN 37 for fifty-five miles, then continue south on IN 58 to reach Bedford.

Totality Duration

3 minutes 43 seconds

Notes

The Bedford city website will have updated announcements of the total eclipse at http://www.bedford.in.us/.

Event	Time (EDT)	Altitude	Azimuth
Sunrise	7:19:00AM	0°	79°
Eclipse Start	1:48:42PM	58°	180°
Totality Start	3:04:41PM	54°	214°
Totality End	3:08:24PM	53°	215°
Eclipse End	4:22:16PM	43°	238°
Sunset	8:16:00PM	0°	280°

Bloomington

Elevation: 771 feet
Population: 85,071
Main road/hwy: I-40

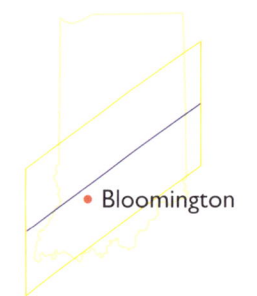

Overview

Founded in 1818 by a group of settlers, Bloomington is located in scenic Monroe County. While the city boasts of tourist attractions such as the WonderLab Science Museum and Wylie House, one can also enjoy an escape from the everyday routine. Go camping at the Charles Deam Wilderness, spend a weekend rejuvenating in a yurt at the Tibetan Mongolian Buddhist Cultural Center, or have a family vacation at Jellystone Park near Lake Monroe. You can fish at the Red Rabbit Inn. Should you return in September, you can attend the Lotus World Music and Arts Festival.

Getting There

Drive southwest from Indianapolis on IN 37 for forty-three miles to reach the city of Bloomington.

Totality Duration

4 minutes 2 seconds

Notes

Visit the city's website for updated information at https://bloomington.in.gov/.

Event	Time (EDT)	Altitude	Azimuth
Sunrise	7:18:00AM	0°	79°
Eclipse Start	1:49:04PM	58°	180°
Totality Start	3:04:45PM	54°	213°
Totality End	3:08:47PM	53°	215°
Eclipse End	4:22:22PM	43°	238°
Sunset	8:17:00PM	0°	280°

Bluffton

Elevation:	813 feet
Population:	10,003
Main road/hwy:	US 65

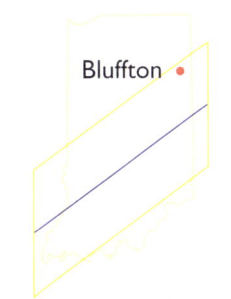

Overview

Nicknamed as the Parlor City nearly a century ago because of the paved streets (a new phenomenon back then), the city offers iconic places to visit. Whether you want to spend the day at the Angel of Hope Memorial Park, remembering a loved one who passed away, or wish to spend time in solitude among books at the most recognized public library in the country, you have it all here. Naturalists will delight in fishing at the Kunkel Lake at the Ouabache State Park, walking among native greenery at the recently reforested Native Habitat Waterway, or enjoying a stroll or bicycle ride at the River Greenway.

Getting There

Drive south from Fort Wayne on IN 1 for twenty-five miles to reach Bluffton.

Totality Duration

2 minutes 30 seconds

Notes

Visit the Parlor City's website for eclipse, travel, and lodging information at https://blufftonindiana.net/.

Event	Time (EDT)	Altitude	Azimuth
Sunrise	7:11:00AM	0°	79°
Eclipse Start	1:53:13PM	56°	184°
Totality Start	3:08:52PM	51°	216°
Totality End	3:11:22PM	51°	217°
Eclipse End	4:24:40PM	41°	238°
Sunset	8:13:00PM	0°	280°

Columbus

Elevation: 630 feet
Population: 47,143
Main road/hwy: IN 46

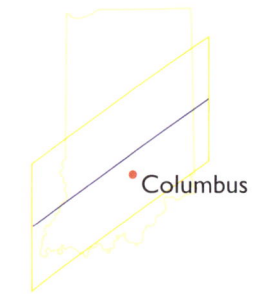

Overview

The city of Columbus in Bartholomew County is one of the greatest places to visit for the connoisseur of architecture. If you choose to take a tour around the city, you should certainly visit the Miller House and Garden, the McDowell Education Center, the North Christian Church, the New Brownsville Bridge, the Bartholomew County Courthouse, the Cerealine Building, and the Prall House. And should you desire to spend some time amidst greenery, you may be overwhelmed by choices among the nearly two hundred and eighty parks that the city has to offer while viewing the total eclipse.

Getting There

Drive south from Indianapolis on the I-65 for forty-three miles, then turn east on IN 46 and drive two miles to reach Columbus.

Totality Duration

3 minutes 45 seconds

Notes

Visit Columbus's website to find out about events the city is hosting for the total eclipse at https://columbus.in.us/.

Event	Time (EDT)	Altitude	Azimuth
Sunrise	7:16:00AM	0°	79°
Eclipse Start	1:50:02PM	58°	182°
Totality Start	3:05:49PM	53°	215°
Totality End	3:09:35PM	53°	216°
Eclipse End	4:23:09PM	42°	238°
Sunset	8:14:00PM	0°	280°

Connersville

Elevation:	823 feet
Population:	12,866
Main road/hwy:	I-40

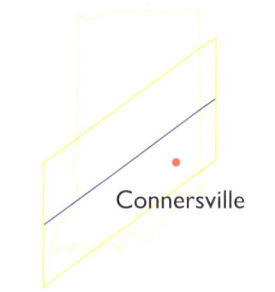

Overview

Whether you are a lover of art, history, or nature, Connersville will not disappoint you. From housing the Fayette County Public Library, the Willowbrook Country Club golf course, and the indoor movie theater, it is the perfect place to spend some pre- or post-eclipse time. You can visit the Canal House and the heritage Whitewater Valley Railroad, which once formed a natural trade route for natives and early settlers. And if you want to enjoy exotic birds flying around, you can take a trip to the Mary Gray Bird Sanctuary.

Getting There

Drive southeast from Indianapolis on I-74 for thirty miles, then turn east on IN 44 and continue for seventeen miles to reach Connersville.

Totality Duration

3 minutes 45 seconds

Notes

The Connersville Community website is a good starting point for travel and hotel information for the total eclipse. Visit their site at http://connersvillecommunity.com/.

Event	Time (EDT)	Altitude	Azimuth
Sunrise	7:12:00AM	0°	79°
Eclipse Start	1:51:49PM	57°	184°
Totality Start	3:07:22PM	52°	216°
Totality End	3:11:07PM	52°	217°
Eclipse End	4:24:18PM	41°	239°
Sunset	8:12:00PM	0°	280°

Evansville

Elevation: 387 feet
Population: 118,930
Main road/hwy: US 41

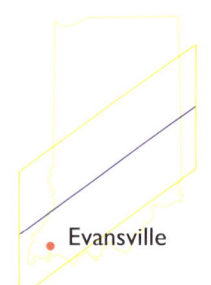

Overview

Found in Vanderburgh County, Evansville is one of the most promising business centers due to its rapid economic growth. Industries growing in Evansville include education, manufacturing, finance, and healthcare. Many transport systems like roads and railways are created to facilitate trade. It is also a home of entertainment with the many entertainment venues such as Ford Center, Victory Theatre, and Bosse Field. If you are an animal lover, you will certainly not want to miss the Howell Wetlands, the Harmonie State Park, the Hovey Lake, and the Wesselman Woods Nature Preserve.

Getting There

Drive southwest on IN 36 to Bloomington, then continue southwest on I-69 to reach Evansville.

Totality Duration

3 minutes 4 seconds

Notes

Evansville's website will have eclipse event information at https://www.visitevansville.com/.

Event	Time (CDT)	Altitude	Azimuth
Sunrise	6:24:00AM	0°	80°
Eclipse Start	12:45:47PM	59°	177°
Totality Start	2:02:29PM	55°	212°
Totality End	2:05:33PM	55°	213°
Eclipse End	3:20:23PM	44°	237°
Sunset	7:20:00PM	0°	280°

Greencastle

Elevation:	843 feet
Population:	10,529
Main road/hwy:	US 231

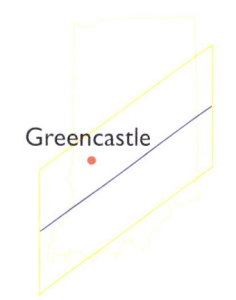

Overview

Surrounded by farmland, the city of Greencastle offers a unique blend of opportunities for recreation. Beer lovers should not miss visiting the Wasser Brewing Company. Gamers will love to visit the Game Warehouse. Should you want to shop for high-quality handmade products, visit Conspire: Contemporary Craft, a retail boutique. If you visit Evansville during other times of the year, you can attend events such as the Annual Greencastle Music Fest, First Friday Greencastle, Monon Bell Game, and the Putnam County 4-H Fair.

Getting There

Drive southwest from Indianapolis for thirty-nine miles, then exit on US 231 and continue north for eight miles to reach Greencastle.

Totality Duration

3 minutes 17 seconds

Notes

Point your web browser to Greencastle's website at https://cityofgreencastle.com/ for updated total eclipse events and lodging information.

Event	Time (EDT)	Altitude	Azimuth
Sunrise	7:19:00AM	0°	80°
Eclipse Start	1:49:14PM	57°	180°
Totality Start	3:05:04PM	53°	213°
Totality End	3:08:22PM	53°	214°
Eclipse End	4:22:10PM	43°	237°
Sunset	8:19:00PM	0°	280°

Indianapolis

Elevation:	715 feet
Population:	872,680
Main road/hwy:	Multiple

Overview

Indianapolis is the capital of the state of Indiana, and while it has thriving insurance, leasing, finance, education, real estate, and rental industries, there's a lot more to the city. This thriving center of the state is active and growing. You can take a three-hour Brewery Tour, visit the Indiana Historical Society, Madame Walker Theatre, and the Eiteljorg Museum. Take the kids to the Indianapolis Zoo, White River State Park, Fort Harrison, and check out the Veal's Ice Tree. And if you want to stay the night overlooking the Monon Trail, you can buy a night at the Hotel Broad Ripple.

Getting There

Indianapolis is a major city and can be reached by car, plane, or bus.

Totality Duration

3 minutes 48 seconds

Notes

The Indianapolis website will have travel, safety, and other eclipse-related information at http://www.indy.gov.

Event	Time (EDT)	Altitude	Azimuth
Sunrise	7:16:00AM	0°	79°
Eclipse Start	1:50:27PM	57°	181°
Totality Start	3:05:58PM	53°	214°
Totality End	3:09:46PM	52°	215°
Eclipse End	4:23:06PM	42°	238°
Sunset	8:16:00PM	0°	280°

Jasper

Elevation: 466 feet
Population: 15,519
Main road/hwy: US 231

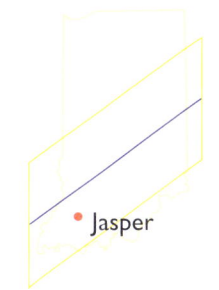

Overview

One of the most fascinating things to do in the city of Jasper is to take the Spirit of Jasper Train, a luxury excursion where you can spend time learning about the city history in train cars. Visit their website at http://spiritofjasper.com. If you wish to spend some quiet time in the presence of nature, you have several options. The Buffalo Trace and Ruxer Golf Courses, Jasper Municipal Swimming Pool, and the Jasper Youth Sports Complex will delight the sportsperson in you. And if you wish to engage in some active art exploration, the Jasper Arts Center is the place to visit.

Getting There

Drive south from Indianapolis on IN 37 for fifty-five miles to the I-69. Then continue southwest on US 23, then drive south to reach Jasper.

Totality Duration

3 minutes 13 seconds

Notes

The city of Jasper website, https://www.jasperindiana.gov/, will have total eclipse lodging and event updates.

Event	Time (EDT)	Altitude	Azimuth
Sunrise	7:21:00AM	0°	80°
Eclipse Start	1:47:22PM	59°	179°
Totality Start	3:03:48PM	54°	213°
Totality End	3:07:02PM	54°	214°
Eclipse End	4:21:27PM	44°	238°
Sunset	8:18:00PM	0°	279°

Marion

Elevation: 810 feet
Population: 28,326
Main road/hwy: US 65

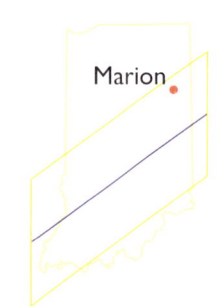

Overview

Marion is found in Grant County and is the seat of Grant County. It is known as the Home of the Hog, a local name for large motorcycles. Every year an event called the Hog Daze is held in downtown Marion, bringing in bike fans from all over the state. Marion city has a rich history, as it is only a few miles from the historical site of the Battle of Mississinewa, a battle between the United States and Native Indians. Thousands of people flock to Marion in the fall to watch the reenactment.

Getting There

Drive north on I-69 from Indianapolis to IN 18. Turn west and drive six miles to reach Marion.

Totality Duration

2 minutes 5 seconds

Notes

Marion's city website, https://cityofmarion.in.gov/, will have multiple business and event links for the total eclipse.

Event	Time (EDT)	Altitude	Azimuth
Sunrise	7:14:00AM	0°	80°
Eclipse Start	1:52:16PM	57°	183°
Totality Start	3:08:14PM	52°	215°
Totality End	3:10:19PM	51°	216°
Eclipse End	4:24:01PM	41°	238°
Sunset	8:15:00PM	0°	279°

Muncie

Elevation:	932 feet
Population:	68,625
Main road/hwy:	US 64

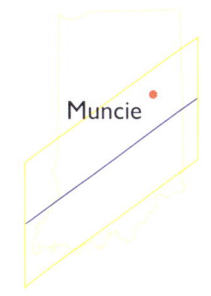

Overview

Originally named Muncietown, later shortened to Muncie in 1845, this vibrant college and manufacturing city is one of the most studied municipalities in America. Ball State, Muncie's college, is a cultural center for the region. The David Owsley Museum of Art collection has over 11,000 pieces of artwork and is well worth a visit. The city has multiple concerts throughout the year. It also has a large selection of craft breweries. Muncie was home to one of the original eleven charter teams of the National Football League from 1905 to 1925.

Getting There

Drive northeast from Indianapolis on I-69 for forty-eight miles, then continue north on IN 67 to reach Muncie.

Totality Duration

3 minutes 45 seconds

Notes

Visit the Muncie's vibrant and active website, http://www.cityof-muncie.com, for total eclipse updates. Check Ball State's website for additional eclipse events at https://www.bsu.edu.

Event	Time (EDT)	Altitude	Azimuth
Sunrise	7:13:00AM	0°	79°
Eclipse Start	1:52:10PM	57°	184°
Totality Start	3:07:29PM	52°	215°
Totality End	3:11:14PM	51°	217°
Eclipse End	4:24:13PM	41°	238°
Sunset	8:13:00PM	0°	280°

Portland

Elevation: 909 feet
Population: 6,143
Main road/hwy: AR 67

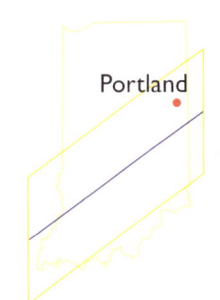

Overview

Portland in Jay County is a city that focuses on providing a friendly environment of facilitating education among its locals. The city is home to a number of historical buildings with amazing architecture, including a courthouse with a dome covered in murals that tell the rich history of this city. Between its well-known museums, breathtaking countryside and parks, tourists visit Portland to enjoy its rich history. This city indeed has a lot to offer its visitors. It will be worth your time to visit Portland to view the solar eclipse and create unforgettable memories.

Getting There

Drive east on I-69 from Indianapolis, then continue east on IN 67 and IN 28 to reach Portland.

Totality Duration

3 minutes 41 seconds

Notes

Start your visit to Portland by pointing your web browser to https://thecityofportland.net/. The city has a calendar for events.

Event	Time (EDT)	Altitude	Azimuth
Sunrise	7:11:00AM	0°	79°
Eclipse Start	1:53:06PM	57°	185°
Totality Start	3:08:18PM	51°	216°
Totality End	3:12:00PM	51°	217°
Eclipse End	4:24:48PM	41°	239°
Sunset	8:12:00PM	0°	280°

Richmond

Elevation:	981 feet
Population:	35,455
Main road/hwy:	I-70

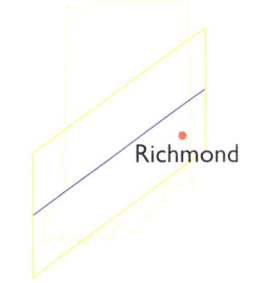

Overview

Richmond lies on the eastern side of Indiana, near the border of Ohio. Richmond gives its wine-loving and antique-enthusiast visitors a variety of antique stores and a winery to visit. It also offers its visitors an all-year-round memorable tour of a self-guided journey through the beautiful and picturesque city. It's full of historic homes, each telling a story about the warm history of Richmond. There is a chocolatier and a variety of bistros and cafés. The magical streets of Richmond will be a beautiful backdrop for the April 8 total solar eclipse.

Getting There

Drive east from Indianapolis for sixty-nine miles on I-70 to reach Richmond.

Totality Duration

3 minutes 49 seconds

Notes

Richmond's website, https://www.richmondindiana.gov/, will have information in its Upcoming Events section.

Event	Time (EDT)	Altitude	Azimuth
Sunrise	7:11:00AM	0°	79°
Eclipse Start	1:52:26PM	57°	185°
Totality Start	3:07:51PM	52°	216°
Totality End	3:11:41PM	52°	218°
Eclipse End	4:24:41PM	41°	239°
Sunset	8:11:00PM	0°	280°

Seymour

Elevation: 604 feet
Population: 19,480
Main road/hwy: US 50

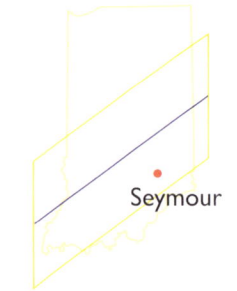

Overview

Famously called the "American Crossroads" because of the intersection of a north-south railroad and an east-west railroad downtown, Seymour is found in the Jackson County. Apart from its historical railroads, Seymour has a variety of beautiful city parks and local theaters to visit, giving tourists an opportunity to appreciate the local talent. The presence of the rail and road system makes it easy for individuals to travel and tour within the area.

Getting There

Drive south from Indianapolis on I-65 for fifty-five miles, then exit onto IN 11 and continue for another five miles to reach Seymour.

Totality Duration

3 minutes 9 seconds

Notes

Check the Seymour city website at http://seymourcity.com/ as a starting place to learn more about eclipse-related events.

Event	Time (EDT)	Altitude	Azimuth
Sunrise	7:16:00AM	0°	79°
Eclipse Start	1:49:45PM	58°	182°
Totality Start	3:05:57PM	53°	215°
Totality End	3:09:06PM	53°	216°
Eclipse End	4:23:04PM	42°	239°
Sunset	8:14:00PM	0°	280°

Terre Haute

Elevation: 499 feet
Population: 60,744
Main road/hwy: I-70

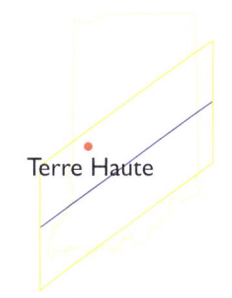

Overview

Terre Haute is situated in Vigo County and is the seat of the county. The city has two airports to ease movement of visitors or locals entering and leaving the city. Terre Haute has a lot to offer its visitors, it is home to a number of art museums, and this is definitely a place full of history that has been preserved over the years. The Clabber Girl Museum features the famous baking powder used by millions of Americans and is worth a visit.

Getting There

Drive southwest on I-70 from Indianapolis for seventy-four miles to reach Terre Haute.

Totality Duration

2 minutes 53 seconds

Notes

Terre Haute's city website, http://www.terrehaute.in.gov/, has event information. It also has a video channel to learn more total eclipse information.

Event	Time (EDT)	Altitude	Azimuth
Sunrise	7:22:00AM	0°	79°
Eclipse Start	1:48:10PM	58°	178°
Totality Start	3:04:18PM	54°	212°
Totality End	3:07:11PM	53°	213°
Eclipse End	4:21:23PM	43°	236°
Sunset	8:21:00PM	0°	280°

Washington

Elevation: 502 feet
Population: 12,114
Main road/hwy: I-69

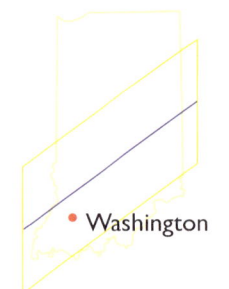

Overview

Founded from the Washington Township, Washington has emerged to be one of the promising cities in Daviess County. This is the best place to visit as it offers a wide variety of activities to its visitors the entire year. Its open landscape would be perfect for viewing the amazing solar eclipse. Tourists can go fishing or boating on the beautiful lakes, or they can hunt for mushrooms in the spring. The Washington Herald newspaper has an events calendar that will provide updates leading up to the total eclipse at https://www.washtimesherald.com/events/.

Getting There

Drive south from Indianapolis on IN 37 to Bloomington, then continue on I-69 to reach Washington.

Totality Duration

3 minutes 58 seconds

Notes

Washington's city website, https://www.washingtonin.us/, has a breaking news note that will keep visitors updated on total eclipse events.

Event	Time (EDT)	Altitude	Azimuth
Sunrise	7:21:00AM	0°	79°
Eclipse Start	1:47:23PM	58°	178°
Totality Start	3:03:19PM	54°	212°
Totality End	3:07:18PM	54°	214°
Eclipse End	4:21:18PM	44°	237°
Sunset	8:19:00PM	0°	280°

Brown County State Park

Elevation: 1,060 feet
Main road/hwy: IN 46

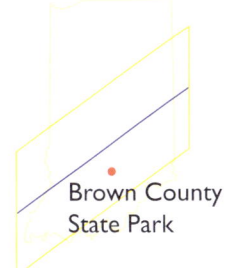

Overview

Brown County State Park has a total area of nearly sixteen thousand acres and is in the southern part of Indiana. It is the largest park in the Hoosier State and receives more than one million visitors per year. It has a beautiful, vast open land for hikers or horseback-riding enthusiasts. It also has a variety of picnic areas, shelters, and a swimming pool, all features that would make family outings memorable. With a clear view of the sky, it will be an enjoyable outdoor place to view the total solar eclipse on April 8, 2024.

Getting There

Drive south from Indianapolis on I-65 to Columbus, then continue west on IN 46 to reach the northern edge of the park.

Totality Duration

3 minutes 55 seconds (Gnaw Bone total eclipse time)

Notes

Refer to the park's website for updates at https://www.browncountystatepark.net/.

Times are for Gnaw Bone and vary depending on position.

Event	Time (EDT)	Altitude	Azimuth
Sunrise	7:17:00AM	0°	80°
Eclipse Start	1:49:37PM	58°	181°
Totality Start	3:05:20PM	58°	214°
Totality End	3:09:16PM	53°	216°
Eclipse End	4:22:49PM	42°	238°
Sunset	8:16:00PM	0°	280°

Green-Sullivan State Forest

Elevation: 594 feet
Main road/hwy: IN 54/159

Overview

Located in Dugger County, Greene–Sullivan State Forest was established in 1936 and occupies more than three thousand acres of land. The amazingly peaceful forest has many attractive and beautiful lakes that promote fishing and boating. There is area camping, with an option to either camp outdoors or rent a cabin. It also has an area for horse camping. Green-Sullivan State Forest is a great place to visit in Indiana. The forest has over one hundred lakes for you to fish, offering some of the finest fishing in the state.

Getting There

Drive southwest from Indianapolis on I-70 to IN 59, then continue south to Hoosier, turn onto IN 54 and continue to Dugger, then turn south to IN 159 to reach the state forest.

Totality Duration

4 minutes 2 seconds (Bucktown total eclipse time)

Notes

Visit the forest's website at https://www.stateparks.com/greene-sullivan_state_forest_in_indiana.html for more information.

Times are for the town of Bucktown.

Event	Time (EDT)	Altitude	Azimuth
Sunrise	7:21:00AM	0°	79°
Eclipse Start	1:47:44PM	58°	178°
Totality Start	3:03:31PM	54°	212°
Totality End	3:07:33PM	54°	213°
Eclipse End	4:21:22PM	43°	237°
Sunset	8:19:00PM	0°	281°

Hoosier National Forest

Elevation: Varies
Main road/hwy: US 50/150

Overview

Hoosier National Forest is tucked into the south hills of central Indiana. It will be another option to enjoy the total eclipse in the outdoors in Indiana. It has a wider range of opportunities as well as resources for you to enjoy, such as rolling hills and back-country trails that make it a good place for hiking and camping. Although the forest is smaller compared to the western forests of America, it is the most beautiful forest in Indiana.

Getting There

Drive south from Indianapolis on IN 37 for eighty-six miles to reach the northern section of the forest in Moorestown.

Totality Duration

Multiple depending on location.

Notes

The southern portion of the forest is *outside* the totality. Visit the forest's website at https://www.fs.usda.gov/hoosier/ for more information.

Times are for the town of Moorestown.

Event	Time (EDT)	Altitude	Azimuth
Sunrise	7:19:00AM	0°	79°
Eclipse Start	1:48:17PM	58°	180°
Totality Start	3:04:23PM	54°	213°
Totality End	3:08:00PM	54°	215°
Eclipse End	4:22:01PM	43°	238°
Sunset	8:17:00PM	0°	280°

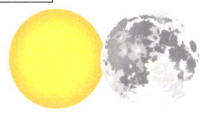

Mounds State Park

Elevation: 879 feet
Main road/hwy: IN 9

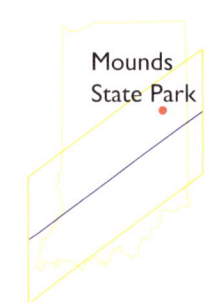

Overview

Mounds State Park may be one of the most interesting areas in Indiana to view the total eclipse from. The ancient earthworks from the Adena-Hopewell people are protected at this park. There are ten earthen mounds, the largest of which is called the Great Mound. Archaeologists theorize that these mounds were places of worship and astronomical observations. What better place could there be to view a total eclipse than an ancient mound site dedicated to heavenly viewing?

Getting There

Follow the same directions as Anderson from Indianapolis. From the intersection of IN 9 and IN 32, drive east on Mounds Road to reach the state park.

Totality Duration

3 minutes 43 seconds

Notes

Visit the park's website at https://www.in.gov/dnr/parklake/2977.htm for access information during the total eclipse.

Event	Time (EDT)	Altitude	Azimuth
Sunrise	7:14:00AM	0°	79°
Eclipse Start	1:51:42PM	57°	183°
Totality Start	3:07:05PM	52°	215°
Totality End	3:10:48PM	52°	216°
Eclipse End	4:23:54PM	41°	238°
Sunset	8:14:00PM	0°	280°

Remember the Indiana Total Eclipse
April 8, 2024

Who was I with? _____
_____
_____
_____
_____

What did I see? _____
_____
_____
_____
_____
_____
_____
_____
_____

What did I feel? _____
_____
_____
_____
_____
_____
_____
_____

What did the people with me think? _____

Where did I stay? _____

Enjoy Other Books by Aaron Linsdau

50 Jackson Hole Photography Hotspots
This guide reveals the best Jackson Hole photography spots. Learn what locals and insiders know to find the most impressive and iconic photography locations in the United States. This is an excellent companion guide to the *Jackson Hole Hiking Guide*. 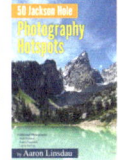
www.sastrugipress.com/books/50-jackson-hole-photography-hotspots/

Adventure Expedition One
by Aaron Linsdau M.S. & Terry Williams, M.D.
Create, finance, enjoy, and return safely from your first expedition. Learn the techniques explorers use to achieve their goals and have a good time doing it. Acquire the skills, find the equipment, learn to camp, understand medical issues, and learn the planning necessary to pull off an expedition. 
www.sastrugipress.com/books/adventure-expedition-one/

Antarctic Tears
Experience the honest story of solo polar exploration. This inspirational true book will make readers both cheer and cry. Coughing up blood and fighting skin-freezing temperatures were only a few of the perils Aaron Linsdau faced. Travel with him on a world-record expedition to the South Pole. 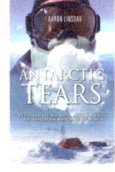
www.sastrugipress.com/books/antarctic-tears/

How to Keep Your Feet Warm in the Cold
Keep your feet warm in cold conditions on chilly adventures with techniques described in this book. Packed with dozens and dozens of ideas, learn how to avoid having cold feet ever again in your outdoor pursuits. 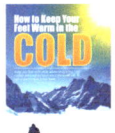
www.sastrugipress.com/books/how-to-keep-your-feet-warm-in-the-cold/

Jackson Hole Hiking Guide
Jackson Hole contains some of the most dramatic and iconic landscapes in the United States. The book shares everything you need to know to hike Jackson's classic trails with canyons, high mountains, and hidden alpine lakes. This book is an excellent companion guide to *50 Jackson Hole Photography Hotspots*. 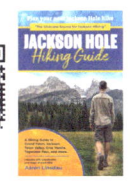
www.sastrugipress.com/books/jackson-hole-hiking-guide/

Subscribe to Aaron's YouTube channel at www.youtube.com/@alinsdau

If you enjoyed this book, please consider leaving a five-star review and a few words on what you liked about it at your favorite online retailer.

Lost at Windy Corner

Windy Corner on Denali has claimed fingers, toes, and even lives. What would make someone brave lethal weather, crevasses, and avalanches to attempt to summit North America's highest mountain? Aaron Linsdau shares the experience of climbing Denali alone and how you can apply the lessons to your life.
www.sastrugipress.com/books/lost-windy-corner/

The Motivated Amateur's Guide to Winter Camping

Winter camping is one of the most satisfying ways to experience the wilderness. It is also the most challenging style of overnighting in the outdoors. Learn 100+ tips from a professional polar explorer on how to winter camp safely and be comfortable in the cold.
www.sastrugipress.com/books/the-motivated-amateurs-guide-to-winter-camping/

Two Friends and a Polar Bear
by Terry Williams, M.D. & Aaron Linsdau

This story of friendship is about two old friends who plan to ski across the Greenland Ice Cap along the Arctic Circle in hopes of becoming one of the oldest teams to succeed.
www.sastrugipress.com/books/two-friends-and-a-polar-bear/

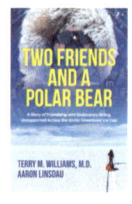

About the Author

Aaron Linsdau is the second American to ski alone from the coast of Antarctica to the South Pole (730 miles / 1174 km), setting a world record for surviving the longest expedition ever for that trip. He lead a 310-mile (499 km) ski expedition across the Greenland icecap along the Arctic Circle. Aaron has climbed Denali solo, crossed the Greenland tundra alone, skied across Yellowstone National Park solo, trekked through the Sahara desert, and successfully climbed Mt. Kilimanjaro and Mt. Elbrus in Russia.

Aaron Linsdau at the South Pole.

Use your smart device to scan the QR codes for website links.

Visit www.aaronlinsdau.com/subscribe to learn more about the author. Receive updates when he releases new books and shows.

Visit Sastrugi Press on the web at www.sastrugipress.com to purchase the above titles in bulk. They are available in print, e-book, or audiobook form.

Thank you for choosing Sastrugi Press.

Enjoy Other Books by Sastrugi Press

50 Florida Wildlife Hotspots by Moose Henderson Ph.D.
This is a definitive guide to finding where to photograph wildlife in Florida. Follow the guidance of a professional wildlife photographer as he takes you to some of the best places to see wildlife in the Sunshine State.
www.sastrugipress.com/books/50-florida-wildlife-hotspots/

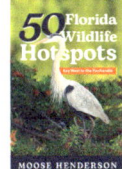

50 Wildlife Hotspots Grand Teton National Park by Moose Henderson Ph.D.
Find out where to find animals and photograph them in Grand Teton National Park from a professional wildlife photographer. Learn techniques, timing, animal behavior, and composition to create stunning wildlife images.
www.sastrugipress.com/books/50-wildlife-hotspots/

Alaska: A Guide for the Curious by Nikki Mann & Jeff Wohl
Discover the natural world of Alaska. Find out what the plants and animals are like, how to identify them, and what the environment of Alaska is like.
www.sastrugipress.com/books/alaska-a-guide-for-the-curious/

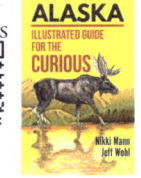

Blood Justice by Tim W. James
Two brothers, one a preacher's son, the other an adopted would-be slave, set out in opposite directions to avenge their family's murder only to cross paths in pursuit of the killer. Book 1 of the Roger Brinkman Series.
www.sastrugipress.com/iron-spike-press/blood-justice/

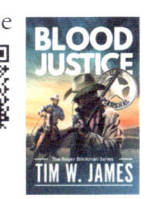

Shake Yourself Free by Bob Millsap
Learn how to overcome difficult encounters with misfortune, tragedy, and loss. Emotional recovery is a journey requiring a mindset shift. Get this book now and take control of your life.
www.sastrugipress.com/books/shake-yourself-free/

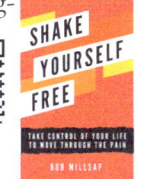

The Burqa Cave by Dean Petersen
Still haunted by Iraq, a retired soldier seeks solace teaching high school in Wyoming. He soon finds the quiet town is home to murderers, maniacs, and a boy who can see where missing murder victims are. This paranormal thriller-romance surprises readers with unexpected twists.
www.sastrugipress.com/books/the-burqa-cave/

Photography Notes

April 8, 2024

Settings _____

_____
_____
_____
_____

Successes _____

_____
_____
_____
_____
_____
_____
_____
_____

Challenges _____

_____
_____
_____
_____
_____
_____

Photography Notes

April 8, 2024

Camera _____

_____
_____
_____
_____

Company _____

_____
_____
_____
_____
_____
_____
_____

Location _____

_____
_____
_____
_____
_____
_____
_____

Made in United States
Troutdale, OR
02/29/2024